TREASURED MOMENTS

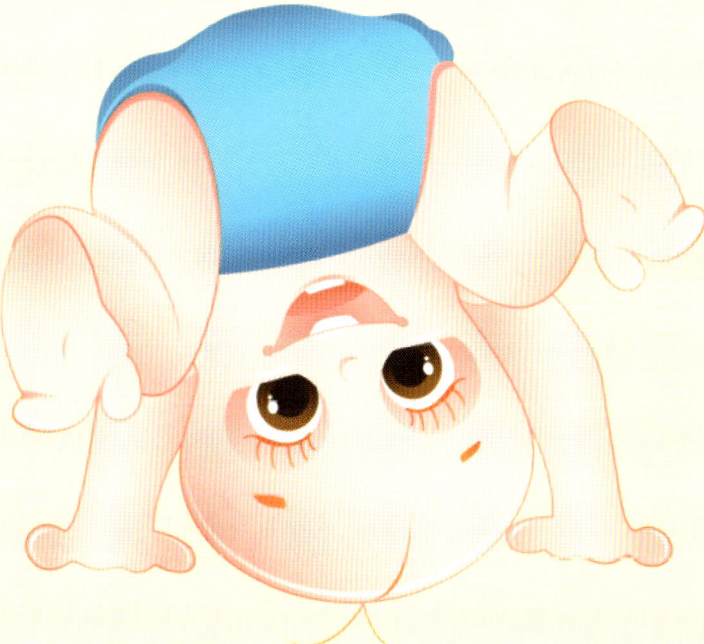

Dr Arun Wadhwa, M.D.

Dr Taruna Wadhwa, M.D.

Viva Books

New Delhi | Mumbai | Chennai | Kolkata | Bengaluru | Hyderabad | Kochi | Guwahati

Publisher's note

First Published 1998

Second Edition 2007

Third Edition 2013

Viva Books Private Limited

- 4737/23, Ansari Road, Daryaganj, New Delhi 110 002
  Tel. 42242200, 23258325, 23283121, Email: vivadelhi@vivagroupindia.net
- 76, Service Industries, Shirvane, Sector 1, Nerul, Navi Mumbai 400 706
  Tel. 27721273, 27721274, Email: vivamumbai@vivagroupindia.net
- Megh Tower, Old No. 307, New No. 165, Poonamallee High Road, Maduravoyal, Chennai 600 095, Tamil Nadu
  Tel. 23780991, 23780992, Email: vivachennai@vivagroupindia.net
- B-103, Jindal Towers, 21/1A/3 Darga Road, Kolkata 700 017
  Tel. 22816713, Email: vivakolkata@vivagroupindia.net
- 7, GF, Sovereign Park Aptts., 56-58, K. R. Road, Basavanagudi, Bengaluru 560 004
  Tel. 26607409, Email: vivabangalore@vivagroupindia.net
- 101-102, Moghal Marc Apartments, 3-4-637 to 641, Narayanguda, Hyderabad 500 029
  Tel. 27564481, Email: vivahyderabad@vivagroupindia.net
- First Floor, Beevi Towers, SRM Road, Kaloor, Kochi 682 018
  Tel. 0484-2403055, 2403056, Email: vivakochi@vivagroupindia.net
- 232, GNB Road, Beside UCO Bank, Silpukhuri, Guwahati 781 003
  Tel. 0361-2666386, Email: vivaguwahati@vivagroupindia.net

www.vivagroupindia.com

ISBN: 978-81-309-2308-6

Published by Vinod Vasishtha for Viva Books Private Limited, 4737/23 Ansari Road, Daryaganj, New Delhi 110 002.

Printed & bound at EIH Limited - Unit Printing Press, Manesar.

This book belongs to

....

Contents

Here is a complete baby book to record your child's daily achievements and the joys you share together in all the moments of life. You will find short and precise guidelines to give you a ready reference which should supplement and not substitute your paediatrician's advice. Record the daily development, milestones, festivals, holidays and outings in the pages provided for that purpose, and of course you must not forget the photographs. Some details may appear superfluous or irrelevant now, but imagine the pleasure when you go through the book ten years later. Or imagine the happiness of your child (then a teenager) when he compares his foot with the footprints you recorded at birth. So get started and enjoy every step, every mood of your child and treasure your memories and cherished moments in this book.

Wishing you a happy and fulfilling parenthood.

Dear new parents, do you remember those long Sunday mornings with newspapers sliding from the bed? Do you remember leisurely summer lunches – the chilled beer and the bee-loud silences? Do you remember impulse trips to a restaurant, to friends, to see a movie? Best forget them for a while and concentrate on the disorderly, demanding, totally unpredictable, unspeakably loud delights of parenthood. One day the quietness will be given back to you and you will have to learn to love it once again.

Pam Brown

Expecting

When was pregnancy discovered? ....

and how? ....

Mother's reaction ....

Father's feelings ....

Consultant, hospital ....

Expected date of delivery ....

Problems during pregnancy if any ....

....

Any fears ....

Mother thought it was a boy or girl ....

Names thought of

For boys ....

For girls ....

Paste ultrasound scan photograph

Photograph

Baby is first photographed

Date of scan .... Baby's age in weeks ....

Congratulations

a tiny baby sweet and new
makes the biggest dream come true

It's a baby .... News given by ....

Born on .... the .... of ...., ...
(day) (date) (month) (year)

.... days before/after due date. Time of birth .... a.m./p.m.

Birth weight .... kg (................................ lb)

Length .... cm Head circumference .... cm

Colour of eyes .... hair ....

Complexion .... Special marks ....

Born at .... , ...
(Hospital) (City)

By normal delivery/forceps/vacuum/caesarean section

Obstetrician ....

Paediatrician ....

People waiting outside the labour room ....

....

First Response of

Mother .... Father ....

Grandparents...

The baby said: To my eyes the world is filled with sweet surprise!

People who visited the baby at the hospital ....

....

....

Majority opinion that the baby resembles ....

First ritual performed by ....

First clothes ....

Residence address and phone nos. when the baby was born ....

....

....

The world as it stood on that day

News headlines of the day ....

....

....

....

Day's temperature .... Rainfall ....

President of the country ....

Prime Minister of the country ....

Political party in power ....

Other important people ....

....

Sports heroes ....

President of America ....

Most popular movie of the time ....

Most popular actor and actress ....

Most popular song and singer ....

Popular TV show ....

Men's fashion ....

Women's fashion ....

Price of common items

Bread .... 500 g butter ....

1 dozen eggs .... Newspaper ....

1 litre petrol .... 10 g gold ....

Bottle of cold drink .... 1 litre milk ....

Common shares and prices ....

.... Index ....

Exchange rates

Dollar .... Pound sterling .... Euro ....

Baby's first photograph

Photograph

Date .... Time .... Age ....

Photograph

Father

Photograph

Mother

Photographs with relatives

Photograph

Date .... Time .... Seen in the picture ....

Photograph

Date .... Time .... Seen in the picture ....

What is normal for a newborn

Babies: A loud noise at one end and no sense of responsibility at the other

The newborn baby weighs 2500 g to 4000 g and measures 45 to 56 cm in length with a head circumference of 33 to 36 cm. The average boy weighs 250 g more than the average girl. The term or mature baby is one born between 37 and 42 weeks of gestation. During the first 3–5 days, the baby loses upto 10 per cent of the birth weight and regains it by the eighth to twelfth day. Although size at birth bears some correlation with future height and weight, exact prediction cannot be made.

The head at birth may have an oblong shape depending on the mode of delivery and consists of relatively soft bones joined by soft tissue. These joints may be prominent, which is normal. There is a diamond-shaped soft depression at the centre of the head (anterior fontanelle) which closes completely by the age of 18 months. There is an unexplained tendency of some infants to prefer lying on one side leading to flattening of that side. It increases to a maximum towards the ninth month, after which it becomes symmetrical in two years.

The mature newborn can see upto a distance of 25 cm (10 inches) from the first day of life and can consistently follow moving objects by six weeks of age. Sub-conjunctival hemorrhage is a bright red patch in the white of the eye or sometimes forming a red ring around the black portion. It is not of serious significance and disappears in two to three weeks.

Round, thickened areas are often present at the midline of the upper lip and are known as sucking blisters. Epithelial Pearls are small white areas present at the roof of the mouth. They are of no significance. True tongue tie is uncommon. If it leads to limitation of movement or sucking, it should be treated with a minor surgical incision. Eruption of one or more teeth before or soon after birth occurs once in 2000 births. If the tooth is loose or interferes with feeding it should be removed.

Skin colour varies widely and depends on the state of circulation of blood. It is pink while asleep and deep red when crying. In the first 48 hours, blueness of hands and feet is very common. It can be an indication that the baby has not been kept warm enough. At birth there can be a protective cheesy covering over the skin called vernix caseosa. If not wiped away it comes off by itself within three to four days. Superficial peeling of skin is common in the first week especially in babies born beyond the due date. Oil massage helps. There can be fine facial and body hair called lanugo. They are gradually lost during the first month. Scalp hair is also gradually lost till five months of age after which a fresh crop appears.

Jaundice is the yellow colouration of skin and white of the eye. Normal (physiological) jaundice appears in 60 to 70 per cent of all newborns. It is first seen after 48 hours and disappears within 10 to 14 days. However, if in doubt, a bilirubin test should be done and values above 12 mg/dl should be taken seriously.

Milia are whitish pin-head-sized spots mainly on and around the nose. They disappear in a few weeks. A bluish black coloration of the skin is often present at the back and buttocks. They are called Mongolian patches and disappear by one year. Erythema toxicum is a common newborn red rash appearing after the second day. Although alarming in appearance, it is harmless and disappears in a few days. Breast engorgement in newborns due to hormonal imbalance is common after the third day. It should not be squeezed or massaged as it subsides by itself in 15 to 30 days.

The newborn shows a few reflex responses which are normal. Grasp reflex is the strong grip by which babies hold on to you when you offer your finger. The tight grip disappears after a few days although they can hold on to objects lightly. The newborn makes a stepping response when held upright on a flat surface. This also disappears after a few weeks. If the child is born around the due date, there is a good sucking reflex. Gently touch at the corner of the mouth and the baby moves the head in that direction and starts sucking.

For the first few days, the baby passes tarry black coloured stools called meconium. After the third day they become yellow and watery for a day (transitional stools) and then settle to a routine of two to eight semi-solid, pasty stools per day. The stools are usually during or soon after a feed. He will pass urine 15 to 20 times in a day, which is normal. Collection of ants near the newborn's urine does not indicate that he has diabetes. Newborns may commonly sneeze many times in a day. In case of a nasal block normal saline drops can be instilled in the baby's nostrils. The nails of a newborn grow very fast and have to be filed/cut every third or fourth day. Some newborns develop a protrusion at the umbilicus which is called umbilical hernia. This regresses by itself by one year of age, and if it does not, then a minor surgery may be required.

Out of the above, the baby had ....

....

Time of passage of first stool ...., ... hours after birth.

Time of passage of first urine ...., ... hours after birth.

The baby arrives and the world is turned upside down.
How utterly irrelevant are things that
Yesterday seemed vitally important.
This new life outweighs them all.

Family tree

....

Great Grandfather

....

Great Grandmother

....

Grandmother

....

Great Grandfather

....

Great Grandmother

....

Grandfather

....

Father

....

Baby

....

Mother

....

Grandmother

....

Great Grandmother

....

Great Grandfather

....

Grandfather

....

Great Grandmother

....

Great Grandfather

Aunts and Uncles

Father's side

....

....

Mother's side

....

....

Little fingerprints

There used to be so many
Of my fingertips to see,
On furniture and walls and things,
From sticky grubby me!

But if you stop and think a while
You'll see I am growing fast
These little handprints disappear
You can't bring back what's past!
So here's a small reminder
To keep, not wipe away,
Of my hands and how they looked
To make you smile someday!

handprints

Left

Right

Date of impression ....

The study of fingerprints is called Dactylography. It is one of the surest methods of identification of an individual. There are four basic patterns and hundreds of different subvarieties. The basic patterns are Arch, Loop, Whorl and Composite. The chance that fingerprints of two different individuals are identical is less than 1 in 64,000 million.

lock of hair

identification tag of hospital

footprints

Left	Right

Date of impression ....

First visitors
and their blessings

When babies come sweet and
small, the happiness is shared by all.

The best compliment received

The best gifts received

A tiny baby so cute and soft is the best gift from God.

Star signs

ARIES
21 March–20 April
Sign – Ram
Element – Fire
Stone – Diamond
Ambitious, hard-working, forceful but warm-hearted

TAURUS
21 April–20 May
Sign – Bull
Element – Earth
Stone – Emerald
Artistic, loyal, ethical, honest, practical but stubborn

GEMINI
21 May–21 June
Sign – Twins
Element – Air
Stone – Moonstone
Quick, clever, impatient, talkative and optimistic

CANCER
22 June–22 July
Sign – Crab
Element – Water
Stone – Carnelian
Sensitive, determined, persistent, ambitious, responsible and methodical

LEO
23 July–22 August
Sign – Lion
Element – Fire
Stone – Sardonynx
Strong-willed, imaginative, far-sighted and cheerful

VIRGO
23 August–22 September
Sign – Virgin
Element – Earth
Stone – Sapphire
Perfectionist, meticulous, kind, gentle, peace-loving

LIBRA
23 September–22 October
Sign – Scales
Element – Air
Stone – Opal
Strong, bright, determined, charismatic and friendly

SCORPIO
23 October–21 November
Sign – Scorpion
Element – Water
Stone – Topaz
Energetic, shrewd, outgoing, observant and imaginative

SAGITTARIUS
22 November–21 December
Sign – Archer
Element – Fire
Stone – Turquoise
Free thinking, talented, loyal, idealistic, strong and ethical

CAPRICORN
22 December–21 January
Sign – Goat
Element – Earth
Stone – Garnet
Determined, diligent, outgoing, observant and imaginative

AQUARIUS
22 January–20 February
Sign – Water bearer
Element – Air
Stone – Amethyst
Independent, self-confident, reliable, creative, sensitive

PISCES
21 February–20 March
Sign – Fish
Element – Water
Stone – Aquamarine
Intelligent, studious, generous, hard-working and diligent

Baby's sign .... **Element** .... **Stone** ....

Horoscope

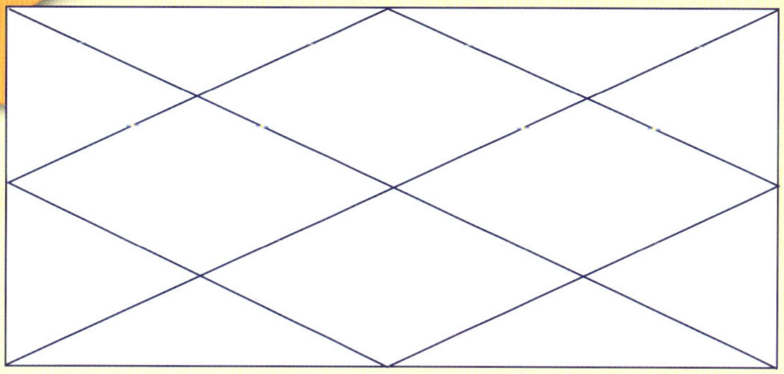

Birthplace ...... Longitude ...... Latitude ......

Name ...... Date of birth ...... Day ......

Vikram Samvat ...... Shali Vahan ...... Christian year ......

Standard time ...... Local time ...... AM ...... RAMC ......

Sun ...... Luna ...... Mars ...... Mercury ......

Jupiter ...... Venus ...... Saturn ...... Node ......

Herschal ...... Neptune ...... Pluto ......

Predictions

......

......

......

......

......

......

......

Parents' hopes and dreams ......

......

......

Hope you grow up best of all
most sought after and loved by all.

Care of the newborn

It feels wonderful to be a parent, overwhelmed by the responsibility of a tiny, delicate and perfect small human being. It takes a large amount of care, patience and energy to bring up a baby. It starts right from the time when the newborn is brought into the room, which may be a couple of hours later in a normal delivery. Handle the baby with tender loving care, always supporting the neck and head whenever you lift the child up. Since the baby cannot regulate its body temperature, keep the room at a constant temperature of 20 to 25°C. Touch the back and tummy of the baby to see if he is comfortable: add/remove the layers of clothing accordingly. You can also keep a watch on the nails of hands and feet – if bluish in colour, then increase warmth, and if they are red (not pink) then remove the clothes. If in doubt measure the temperature of the baby in the armpit using a common thermometer. In newborns it shows the actual temperature and no addition has to be done. In the initial few weeks the baby sleeps 16 to 20 hours a day, sometimes more during day than night, much to the discomfort of the mother. Take a nap when the baby does, rather than rushing with household chores. Relaxation is the key to establishment of good breast feeding in the early weeks.

Start breast feeding as soon as possible. In the first-time mothers, it takes a little longer and may appear impossible but have patience. Initially only a few spoons of whitish yellow sticky fluid (colostrum) is secreted and that is all that the child needs. Proper milk flow is established only by the third day. Don't be tempted to start formula feeds. If you think the baby is not satisfied, consult your doctor. Avoid visitors handling the newborn specially if they have cough or cold. Keep flowers and bouquets away from the baby's cot.

Continue breast feeding the child for at least the first six months. Feeding should be as on demand of the child, which may be every two to four hours and not by the clock. Use alternate breasts each time. The baby should be in a reclining position with head elevated. After every feed put the child on the shoulder and pat firmly till he burps. If there is difficulty in burping, make the child lie on its side. Some babies bring up a little milk after every feed, there is nothing wrong if the baby is growing well and gaining weight. The mother should take a good diet rich in proteins, consisting of milk, cereals, fresh fruits and vegetables. Avoid excessive fatty foods and foods which cause flatulence.

Bathe the baby daily using any of the baby/glycerine soaps. In winters, bath and sponging can be done on alternate days. Since the babies cannot regulate their body temperature make sure that the room is warm and free of draughts. The water should be warm and not hot. Make sure you have collected everything you may need, before you start. Hold the baby inside the water, hand under his arms so that his head is resting in the crook of your arm. Use the other hand to gently trickle the water from the bath-tub. Older children are bathed better on a rubber mat than on the floor as it reduces the chance of an accidental slip.

After the bath, wrap the baby in a soft towel immediately and dab dry taking special care of creases and folds of the skin. After 30 days it is good to massage the child using any oil except mustard oil. Powder if applied should be sprinkled on the palm of your hand and then rubbed on the baby avoiding the creases. Soft cotton clothes should be used. Front open dresses are better as they are easy to manage and buttons don't hurt the child. Cap and woollen shoes are a must in winters. No mohair, angora or brushed yarn please.

The umbilical cord falls off within 4 to 10 days. The base of the stump should be cleaned thrice daily with spirit or any other antiseptic. Never apply talcum powder over it. Avoid using plastic/disposable nappies in the initial few weeks as it may lead to a nappy rash. Do not apply 'kajal' or 'surma' into the eyes or try to clean nose or ears with ear buds. Do not give honey, ghutti or gripe water to the newborn child. The newborn does not need water for the first six months.

A newborn should pass urine and stool at least once in the first 24 hours of life. After the first week a breast-fed infant will pass 2 to 10 pasty stools and urinate 15 to 20 times in a day. Whenever the baby is wet he will signal it by crying and changing position. Nappies should be changed as early as possible, otherwise, the chemical waste in the urine and stool can lead to a nasty nappy rash. Disposable or washable nappies can be used. Although the former are more convenient they are more expensive and can be reserved for outings or during nights. Washable ones should be passed through an antiseptic solution at least once a day. Thorough ironing also helps in their sterilization. Ensure you have collected everything before you begin a change. Always clean from front to back and specially so in girls to prevent spreading of germs from stools into the urinary tract. Some babies may still develop a nappy rash in spite of all precautions. In such a situation keep the area clean and dry (open in summers). Apply a common nappy rash cream after every change.

The only language of communication a baby knows is crying. He may be hungry, wet, feeling cold or hot or just wants to be close to you for a cuddle. If you cannot see a reason, try a change of scene – take him for a stroll or a short drive. Soon you would be able to interpret the different cries. Always see to the need of your baby as soon as possible. By picking up the child each time he cries, you are in no way spoiling his habits. In fact he would develop a better sense of security.

The newborn spends most of the time sleeping, sometimes only for short bursts. Always make him sleep on the back or side. A soft thin pillow can be used. Some babies are born with a reverse sleep cycle – sleeping during the day and playing at night. Nothing much can be done to change the cycle. Fortunately it settles by itself in 6 to 12 weeks.

You will come across a lot of 'experts' who think they know best. You will read books, articles and search the net. In all this concern never lose sight of the guidance of the expert – the baby. Have confidence in your own intuition. Listen to advice but translate it into what you feel is right for your child. Spend maximum time with your baby and involve your husband as much as possible. Get a massage in the morning, rest during day-time and go for long walks in the evening. Accept offers of help and reduce household chores to the minimum. Do regular pelvic exercises and do not diet for six months. Don't worry about the hair loss which is normal after delivery. Lastly, don't forget to date the photographs and complete this book.

Feeding time

In the initial few years, feeding takes an important place in the care of the child. Proper, balanced dietary habits cultivated from infancy continue till late in life. The child should be put on the breast within 3–4 hours of delivery. Initially, only few spoons of clear white sticky fluid (colostrum) is secreted and proper milk is seen only after the third day. Breast milk is the perfect food available at the right temperature at a minute's notice. It has all the nutrients in proper proportion and has antibodies to prevent from common childhood infections. It promotes early bonding between the mother and the child. Contrary to common belief, it helps the mother to come back to her normal shape faster. There is evidence that breast feeding reduces the risk of breast cancer in later life. Till the time the baby is six months old, nothing other than mother's feed is to be given. No top milk, tea, coffee, cold drink, gripe water etc. not even water.

Weaning is the process of gradual transition from mother's milk to solid food by one year of age. After four months if the weight gain is inadequate or the mother has to join work, a top feed can be started. Cereals, especially wheat cereals, should definitely not be given before six months of age. Start with a few spoons of vegetable soup or dal water. Never boil the juice. After a week to ten days give banana or mango mashed in milk. In cereals start first with a rice cereal and next wheat. Initially, the readymade tinned cereals can be given shifting later to natural home food like kheer and porridge (daliya). Salt and sugar are not given till 9 months of age. Citrus juices are best avoided till one year of age.

Egg yellow can be introduced after 6 months and egg-white can be added after 9 months of age. Some children are averse to drinking milk in any

form. The only practical solution is to give milk substitutes like fresh curd, custard, kheer, cheese, etc. Curd has more proteins, calcium, vitamin B-complex and less fat than milk, so it is equally good or perhaps better than milk. Fresh curd (not sour or cold) does not lead to throat/chest infections. A child taking a balanced diet does not require extra vitamins or tonics. A few important points to be remembered are: 1) Start one new feed at a time. Let the child develop a taste and then introduce another new feed. 2) If the child does not like the taste initially, keep trying daily for at least a week before abandoning for next 3 to 4 weeks. 3) Do not force-feed. 4) All new diets should be given in the morning. Any adverse reactions like colic, rashes, etc. can be better managed during the day. 5) Do not give artificially coloured and flavoured sweets and drinks and obviously avoid unhygienic food.

By the time the child is one year old he/she should be on table food diet of dal, mashed vegetables, rice, roti, idli, etc. The feeding time should be a peaceful affair and the child should be encouraged to eat along with others but on his special chair. After one and a half years the child can be trained to feed himself with a spoon. Bottle feeds, if started, should in any case be discontinued after one year of age. If continued beyond one year it leads to inadequate solid feeding, ear infections, dental caries and thumb sucking in later childhood. Bottle feeding is also the commonest cause of recurrent diarrhoea in children.

Given a name

Today .... of ...., ... we the
(date) (month) (year)

board of directors decided to call our darling as ....

The meaning of the name is ....

It was final consensus because ....

The name was chosen amongst the following names proposed

....

....

However, at home we propose to call by any of these love pet names

....

....

Religious ceremony held ....

....

Photograph

Date of Photograph .... Age ....

The first celebration

It was held on .... at ....

No. of people invited .... attended ....

Age of the little one .... Clothes worn ....

Menu

....

....

Party Highlights

....

....

....

....

....

....

....

....

Space for copy of invitation card

Party photographs

Photograph

Seen in the picture L to R ....

Photograph

Seen in the picture L to R ....

First Lohri

The first Lohri was celebrated when .... was .... months old .... relatives and friends were invited. It was very warm and cosy in front of the fire.

....

Photograph

Lohri is a North Indian festival celebrated to mark the arrival of a newborn, new bride, etc. in the family. Bonfire is lit in the evening and sweets/dry-fruits are distributed.

First Holi

This year holi was celebrated on .... It was a welcome change to discard the woollen and play with water and colours. The photograph shows how colourful .... looked.

Reactions of the child ....

....

....

....

Photograph

Holi is a colourful and boisterous festival of our country when all friends, neighbours and relatives forget their difference and greet each other with colour. Children enjoy themselves by throwing coloured water. Care should be taken to use good quality colour. Eyes should be specially protected. Smaller children should be prevented from drenching. Apply a skin protecting cream on face and arms before going out to celebrate. Colour from hair is easy to get rid of if oil is applied beforehand.

Raksha-Bandhan

It is a Hindu festival of North India. Sisters tie the holy thread or rakhi on the wrists of their brothers wishing them long life. Brothers take oath to protect their honour and help them in adverse times. The first rakhi was celebrated on ....

Child's age .... Rakhi tied by/to ...., ...

Photograph

Onam

....

....

....

....

....

....

....

....

Ganeshotsav

Photograph

Durga Puja

Dussehra

Photograph

Diwali

festival of lights

The first Diwali was celebrated on .... the ....
(day) (date)

.... was scared/not scared of all the wild noises.

Relatives who joined us ....

Gifts for the baby ....

Highlights ....

....

Photograph

Deepawali is the brightest Indian festival when every city, town and village is turned into a fairyland with millions of lights, candles and oil lamps, lighting the homes and public buildings. People exchange sweets and greetings. The special feature is the worship of Laxmi, the Goddess of wealth and prosperity.

Eid

Id-ul-Fitr or Ramzan Id is celebrated to mark the end of Ramzan, the holy month of fasting. It is an occasion for feasting, rejoicing and feeding the poor. Id-ul-Zuha or Bakra Id is observed to commermorate Hazrat Ibrahim's offer to sacrifice his son. This year the occasions were on .... and ....

Photograph

Bhai-Dooj

Bhai-dooj or Tikka is celebrated on the second day after Diwali. Sisters apply sacred saffron on the forehead of their brothers and exchange gifts. The first Tikka was on .... Child's age ....

Gurupurab

It is the birth anniversary of Guru Nanak, the first Guru of Sikhs. This year it was celebrated on .... and .... was taken to the .... Gurudwara.

Christmas

It is a Christian festival celebrated on 25th December every year. Santa Claus brings surprise gifts on the X'mas eve.

We visited .... church.

Photograph

Other ceremonies

First haircut

First haircut was done on .... by ....
when .... was .... old.
Highlights ....
....

Photograph

Before

Photograph

After

Mundan is the religious ceremony of completely shaving off the scalp hair, performed at different ages by various communities. Use a new disposable blade and take care to avoid cuts and wounds. It does not lead to increased and better growth of hair, as commonly believed.

First birthday party

The first birthday party was held on ....

The party was at .... and .... people attended.

Birthday cake ....

Party dress ....

Menu ....

Party highlights ....

....

....

Photograph

The best gifts received were ....

....

....

....

People we missed ....

....

Party photographs

Photograph

Photograph

Step by step

With a child at home each day
brings new exciting things

		Age of achievement
6 weeks	Follows moving objects	....
	Smiles back	....
4 months	Rolling side to side	....
	Puts objects into mouth	....
	Pushes with feet when erect	....
6 months	Sitting with support	....
	Transfers objects hand to hand	....
	Enjoys mirror	....
9 months	Moves around the furniture	....
	Waves bye-bye	....
	Responds to name	....
	Throws objects	....
1 year	Monosyllables	....
	Walks with one hand held	....
	Understands 'no' and obeys it	....
	Plays ball game	....
	Postural adjustments to dressing	....
13 months	Walking without support	....
15 months	Crawls up stairs	....
	Makes tower of 3 cubes	....
	Draws a line with crayon	....
	Inserts pellets in a bottle	....
	Indicates desires by pointing	....
18 months	Sits on small chair	....
	Climbs stairs with one hand held	....
	Explores waste baskets	....
	Imitates vertical strokes with crayon	....
	Names pictures	....
	Identifies parts of the body	....

	Kisses when asked	....
	Eat on their own	....
	Pushes wheeled toys	....
2 years	Runs well, opens doors	....
	Goes up and down stairs 1 step at a time	....
	Climbs on furniture and jumps	....
	Speaks three-word sentences	....
30 months	Walks up stairs on alternate foot	....
	Draws a circle	....
	Knows full name	....
	Helps put things away	....
	Wants everything immediately	....
3 years	Tricycle riding	....
	Knows age and sex	....
	Un-buttons clothing	....
	Puts on shoes	....
	Washes hands	....
	Can walk on tiptoe	....
	Knows colours	....
	Questions start – Why? How?	....
4 years	Hops on one foot	....
	Uses scissors to cut pictures	....
	Plays with other children	....
	Draws square and cross	....
	Blows nose reliably	....
	Holds pen properly, draws a man	....
5 years	Draws triangle	....
	Skips	....
	Ten-word sentences	....

The ages mentioned above are average ages and there is a range within which the child should achieve these milestones. Early attainment does not mean that the child is a prodigy, neither does delayed attainment mean that he is of low intelligence as long as it is within the normal limits. The child can be faster in one set of milestones and slower in others. Language is one of the most variable of all and if the child does not have any physical/mental problem, hearing defect, etc., it can be normally delayed. Cause of concern would be if there is delay in more than one milestone beyond the maximum permissible age. If there is lack of comprehension, disinterest in the environment and an absence of quality play, then an expert professional opinion should be sought.

Other milestones

First step .... First ma-ma ....

First success with the potty .... age ....

First fall from bed .... First slap ....

First letter received on .... from ....

First birthday party attended on .... of ....

First toy car ride .... presented by .... on ....

First tricycle ride .... presented by .... on ....

First ride on a scooter ....

In an autorikshaw .... Taxi ....

First visit to a place of worship .... on ....

First Dussehra festival ....

First outing to a market .... on ....

First marriage attended on .... of ....

First movie seen at the cinema hall on ....

Movie .... Hall ....

First maid .... was there till ....

Ear lobe piercing done on ....

First bank account no. .... in bank ....

Opening amount .... Signatories ....

First insurance policy no. .... amount ....

First provident fund account no. ....

Bank/Post Office .... opening amount ....

Other bonds etc. .... presented by ....

First passport made .... no. ....

Baby show attended ....

Prizes won ....

First song ....

First friends ....

....

Favourite Uncle and Aunty ....

Favourite advertisements on TV ....

Favourite song ....

Favourite lullaby ....

Favourite toy/game ....

Afraid of .... but not of ....

Person specially attached to at home ....

In the neighbourhood ....

Favourite pet ....

Baby Language – Early Vocabulary

Age .... Age ....

...**Mum**... meant ...**Water**... .... meant ....

.... meant .... meant ....

.... meant .... meant ....

Other words invented to name common objects or to indicate desires ....

....

....

A typical baby's day

At the age of one month

Sleeping ....

Feeding ....

Mother's impressions ....

....

....

Father's views

....

....

....

....

....

Photograph

At the age of six months

Sleeping ....

Feeding ....

Mother's impressions ....

....

....

Father's views

....

....

....

....

....

Photograph

At the age of one year

Sleeping ....

Feeding ....

Mother's impressions..

....

....

Father's views

....

....

....

....

....

Photograph

At the age of two years

Sleeping ....

Feeding ....

Mother's impressions ....

....

....

Father's views

....

....

....

....

Photograph

Baby moods

Photograph of the child laughing

Date .... Age ....

Photograph of the child crying

Date .... Age ....

Taking a bath

Date .... Age ....

Sleeping

Date .... Age ....

Travel tips

For most parents, staying at home with a child is challenging enough; venturing out with one would give nightmares. Yet, when the open roads and skies beckon, toddler or no toddler, time does come to get up and go. So go, but not before you have planned and planned meticulously.

If the child is more than two years old, consider his likes and dislikes before deciding where to go. His preference would be for open spaces like seaside, while you might prefer museums and art galleries where he might throw a tantrum. Remember, if he doesn't enjoy, nobody else will. One-destination vacations are the most successful. If you are planning a touring vacation, limit the stops. When travelling by plane book early and consider off-peak-time, non-hopping flight. Early booking helps in choosing your seat and also a cradle seat can be asked for. Board as late as possible. To prevent ear block during take-off and landing put the child on bottle/breast. Older child can be given something to chew or suck. Warm towels can be used for fomentation if it actually pains. Remember not to include the lap child in your safety belt – a little impact could injure his stomach and chest. For an older child a car seat can be carried alongwith. While travelling by train or car a travel buggy and a potty can be added to the list. Whatever the mode of travel, carry a good supply of changes, wipes, water, food, medicines and of course camera and charger.

Avoid travelling with a sick child unless it is a must and you have clearance from the treating doctor. The following instructions may help in first aid. The doses can be adjusted according to the child's weight. Syrup Phenergan can be used for motion sickness. It is to be given as 5 ml per 12 kg of child's body weight half an hour before starting the journey.

If the child develops high fever, take him to a cool place and remove all extra clothes. Start sponging the forehead, head and back with tap water. Give paracetamol (Crocin/Calpol/Metacin) approximately 5 ml/10 kg weight and repeat 4–6 hourly if required. If the fever is not coming down, use either Syp Flexon or Combiflam 5 ml/10 kg.

For loose motions start electrolyte solution, coconut water, 'lassi' and 'dal' water. If vomiting is a feature then give Syp Ondem 1 ml/5 kg. Wait for 30 to 40 min before giving any food or fluids. Associated pain in the abdomen can be treated by common anti-spasmodic drops – the Colimex drops 1 dr/kg.

Carry some common medicines for cough and cold and start in usual doses if required. Medicines should be given just before a feed and not after because if the child vomits, the effort of feeding is not wasted. Do remember to carry local antiseptic ointments/band-aid, etc. While travelling, it is better to use powdered milk and mineral water whenever possible.

It is advisable to contact a local paediatrician if cough becomes worse, respiration becomes rapid, fever becomes uncontrollably high or motions and vomiting persist. Your own paediatrician's contact numbers including the STD code should always be with you while travelling.

Travel diary

First outing in a car was on .... Went to ....

Car number .... Make and model ....

First trip outside city limits ....

Went to .... by ....

First picnic on .... to ....

First train journey .... Age ....

Train name and no. .... Went to ....

First bus journey ....

First aeroplane flight .... Age ....

Airline .... Flight no. .... Went to ....

First hill station visited ....

From .... to .... Went by ....

Sites visited ....

....

First experience with boating ....

Ship ....

Reaction at first sight of water ....

Visits abroad ....

Other places seen ....

....

Interesting incidents ....

....

....

The trick to a restful vacation is to keep your expectations low and patience high. Don't forget to pack a lot of sense of humour because if you are able to laugh when things go wrong – as they will – you'll feel half as bad.

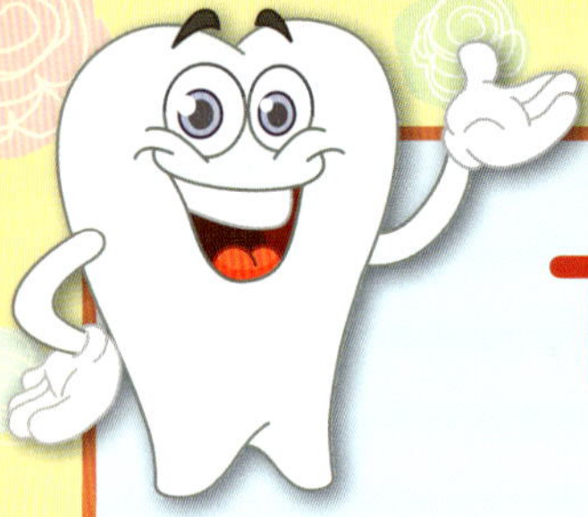

Teething troubles

No.	Name	Avg. age of appearance	Date/age of appearance
1.	Central lower incisors	06–08 months	....
2.	Central upper incisors	08–10 months	....
3.	Lateral upper incisors	12–15 months	....
4.	Lateral lower incisors	12–15 months	....
5.	Upper molars	18–24 months	....
6.	Lower molars	18–24 months	....
7.	Lower canine	18–24 months	....
8.	Upper canine	18–24 months	....
9.	Lower molars	20–30 months	....
10.	Upper molars	20–30 months	....

The teeth start growing within the gums after 2 months of age but they actually erupt anytime after 6 months. The time of appearance of the first tooth can vary from 3 months to 1 year. Early appearance of upper teeth is not a bad omen. Since the teeth start moving in the gums after 2 months of age they may cause discomfort to the child. The baby may be fretful, dribble saliva and bite at everything. He may feel a little warm and sweat a little more, but teething definitely does not cause diarrhoea. At times like this, rub his gums gently with your finger or with any glycerine-based teething gel. Offer him something firm to chew like a carrot, rusk or a soup stick. Teething rings are to be used only if you can ensure their regular cleaning. Once the baby has around ten teeth give him plenty of fresh fruit and vegetables to build up his jaw muscles and start brushing. Sugary foods and chocolates are best avoided. If he must, then remember to give him some water to drink or rinse his mouth.

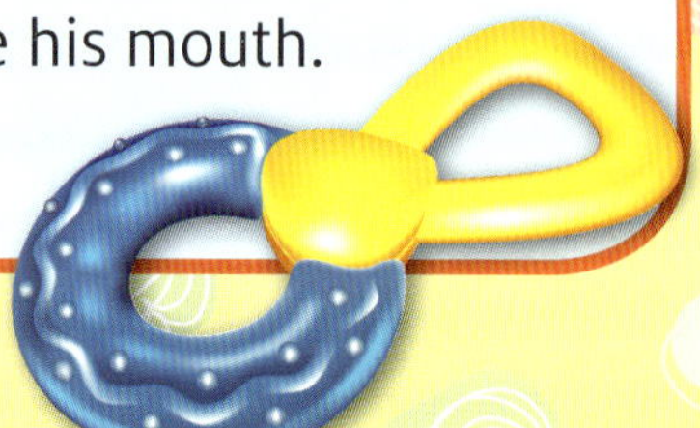

Medical record

Paediatrician at the time of delivery ....

Follow-up visits were with ....

Address .... Phone nos. ....

Alternative doctor ....

Record of visits for purposes other than vaccination:

Date	Illness	Medicine given

Visit to a dentist ....

Visit to other specialists ....

....

Major injury if any ....

Hospitalization if any ....

....

Surgical procedures ....

....

Haemoglobin .... gms/dl on .... Blood group ....

Eyesight .... Hearing .... Blood pressure ....

Allergies ....

Always dress the child in simple clothing which can be easily removed in the clinic.

Common problems

The child is more prone to any kind of infection as compared to an adult because of low body defence mechanisms. For the first two years diarrhoeal disorders are a major problem, whereas in the 2 to 5 years age group respiratory infections take the lead. Cough and cold are the commonest illnesses encountered in the metros especially during changing seasons. As most of them are viral in nature, antibiotics are seldom required. They however need medical attention when the cough becomes very noisy or is associated with breathing difficulty and/or high fever. Viral fever has no specific treatment and only management of symptoms is required. Fortunately it cures by itself in four to five days.

About 5 per cent of all children are prone to developing convulsions at the onset of fever. Do not panic. Remove all extra clothes, sponge the whole body with tap water. Give paracetamol or any other fever medicine immediately after the convulsions have stopped. Consult your doctor at the earliest, specially after the first episode. Children usually grow out of it by the age of 3 years and there are no long-term brain defects.

Stomach infections are characterized by vomiting, loose motions, stomach-ache and sometimes fever. Give some medicine to stop the vomiting and start with plenty of fluids like electrolyte solutions, coconut water, dal water, etc. Do not give glucose water. Stomach-ache should be suspected when the baby cries uncontrollably and is relieved by abdominal massage. Anti-spasmodic drops is all that is required. Some babies have pain at a particular time of the day daily and is popularly known as evening colic. Its exact cause is not known but proper feeding, burping and colic drops help. Hygiene is the cornerstone in prevention of stomach infections. Keep washing the toddler's hands frequently and keep the nails short and clean. Take care that the baby does not put floor litter in his mouth. Bottle-feeding is best avoided, but if you must, the bottle should be boiled for at-least 10 minutes before each feed. Soothers and teething rings are not to be used. Thrush is the white coating

over the tongue seen in bottle-fed infants or after antibiotics. Local application of anti-fungal lotion is required for 5–7 days.

Eye flu or conjunctivitis is a common problem during changing seasons. The eyes are swollen, red and eyelids get stuck together because of thick pus-like discharge. Wash the eyes with cotton swabs soaked in boiled and cooled water and start putting antibiotic eye drop, 1 drop in each eye three-hourly for 5 to 7 days. Ear discharge is a serious problem for which you must consult your paediatrician or ENT surgeon at the earliest. Do not self-medicate by using any eardrops. Dandruff-like greasy scales and peeling of the scalp skin is common in the first six months especially in winters. Severe forms lead to formation of a 'cradle cap'. Gentle washing and cleaning with cetavelon shampoo followed by brushing prevents its worsening to eczema. Urine infection is more common in girls than boys. It can present as unexplained fever or can be associated with increased frequency of urination and excessive crying while passing urine. However, babies, especially boys, may cry before and after passing urine, which is normal. In suspected urinary infection, urine culture and an appropriate antibiotic is required.

With the arrival of a newborn the older child feels emotionally threatened and may show behaviour disturbances leading to sibling rivalry. To avoid such a situation prepare the child before delivery itself. Involve the older child in the care of the sibling, so that he can relate to him with love, responsibility and feeling of belonging. Breath holding spells usually occur between the ages of 6 months and 3 years. The child starts crying after he is hurt, frustrated or frightened. Breath is held for a few seconds and the child becomes blue. Measures should be taken to avoid precipitating factors. The attack can be aborted by using a strong physical stimulus like a pinch, applied at the onset of the spell. It is essential that there is consistency in both the parents' behaviour and they do not reinforce the child's actions after he recovers from the spell. Over-anxiety of parents may lead the child to use it as an attention-seeking disorder. Head banging and rocking in the bed gives the child a pleasurable sensation. Thumb-sucking and nail-biting are also examples

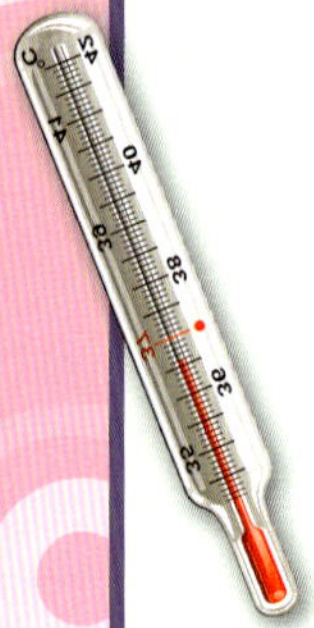

of similar self-stimulation although thumb-sucking is normal during 3 to 9 months. These habits, if persist, can be due to a feeling of insecurity. Patient explanation along with physical prevention can be of help. Teeth-grinding results from tension originating in unexpressed anger or resentments (It is definitely not related to intestinal worms). Helping the child to find ways to express resentment may relieve the problem. Bedtime can be made more enjoyable permitting re-experience and review of some of the fears or angers experienced during the day.

An important aspect in medical care is the parent-doctor relationship. The doctor contributes invaluable technical advice and the parents provide insight into their children. Choose the right physician who is willing to provide you the best care possible. Besides being qualified in paediatrics and having a convenient office location and office hours, he should be responsible, sympathetic and accessible – willing to listen to your concerns, encourage your questions, offer explanations and not grudge the extra time that may be necessary. Of course he has to be good with your children. On your end you should always try and follow the protocol, tell the whole truth, follow the doctor's instructions or clearly explain why you can't. If in doubt, ask for explanation, discuss conflicting advice and when you are unhappy talk directly. The right physician will not mind your calling up even for silly queries and concerns, but unless it is an emergency wait for the office time – he also has a family and some commitment towards it. Whether it is mid-afternoon or midnight, paediatricians spend more time in phone consultations than any other speciality, so prepare yourself before calling. The child's symptoms, temperature, weight, medicines given last time, questions about diet, etc. should be ready along with a working pen and paper. Phone immediately if the child develops fever above 104°C, or it is associated with convulsions, limpness, inconsolable crying, whimpering, purple spots on the body, severe headache, neck stiffness, difficulty in breathing or swallowing. In a newborn, a subnormal temperature is more alarming than fever. Also call urgently if there is bleeding from any site, severe diarrhoea and vomiting, abnormal behaviour or if the child has swallowed any object or medicine.

Growth charts

- The male baby is usually 250 to 500 g heavier and 1 cm longer than the female baby of the same age.
- The weight gain of a newborn is at the rate of 200 g per week in the first three months and 150 g per week in the next three months. At 6 to 9 months age the weight gain reduces to 100 g per week and after 9 months to 75 g a week. Thereafter, the weight increases at the rate of 50 g a week till the child is 10 years old. This explains why the child at one year eats less than what he took at three months.
- The weight of the baby doubles by the fifth month and triples by one year of age.
- The approximate height a child may achieve can be calculated. Add the parents' height in centimetres and add 13 for boys (or subtract 13 for girls) and divide the total by 2.
- The newborn at birth measures 50 cm and doubles its height by 4 years.
- The height at 1 year 10 months is approximately half of adult height.
- There are various factors which determine the ultimate height and weight achieved by a child – the most important being heredity. As long as the child's parameters show a steady increase and fall within the normal range (colour zones), there is no cause for worry. Consult your doctor if your child's growth curve falls in the white zone as shown in the graph overleaf.

Length, weight and head circumference for BOYS from 0–36 months

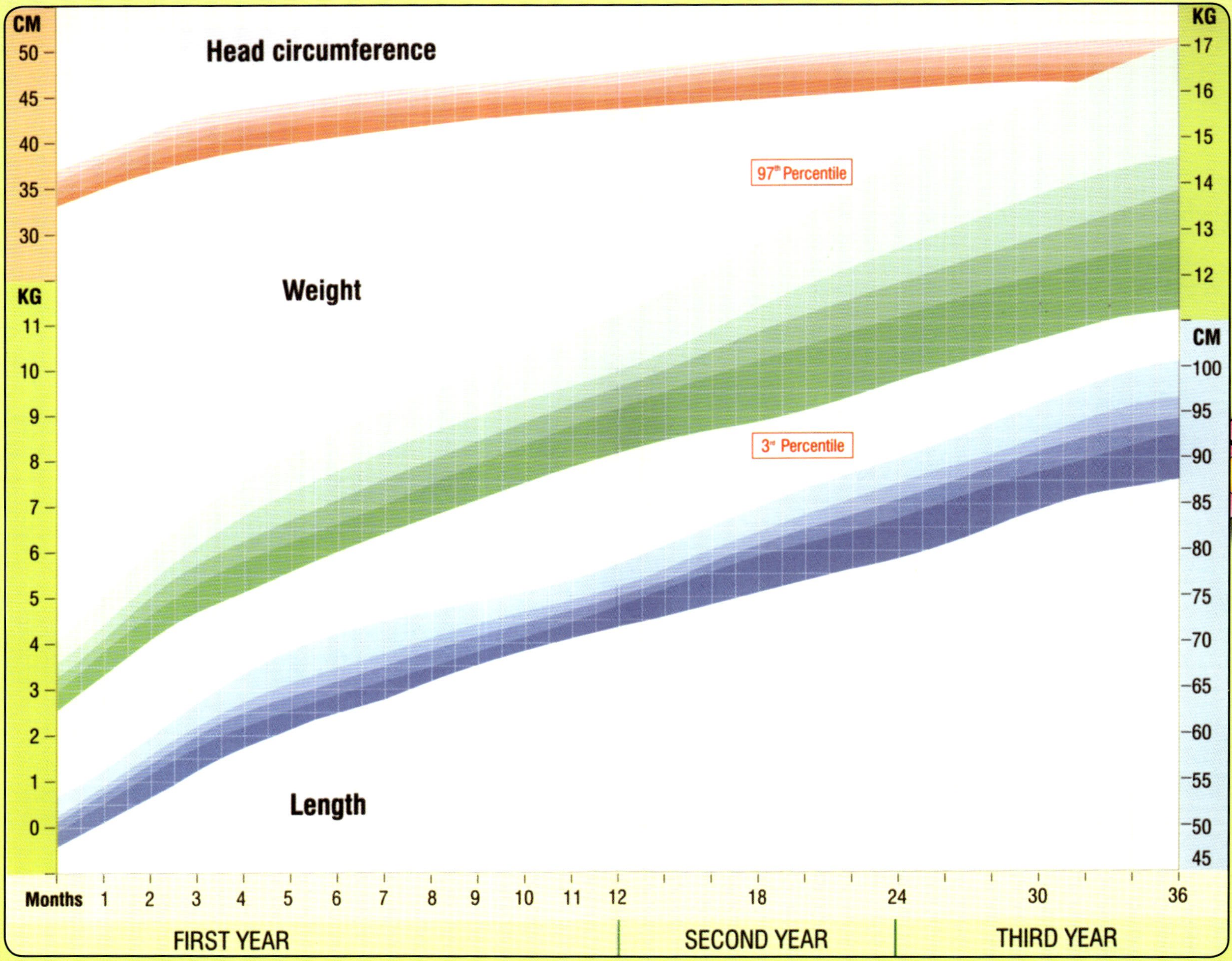

Length, weight and head circumference for GIRLS from 0–36 months

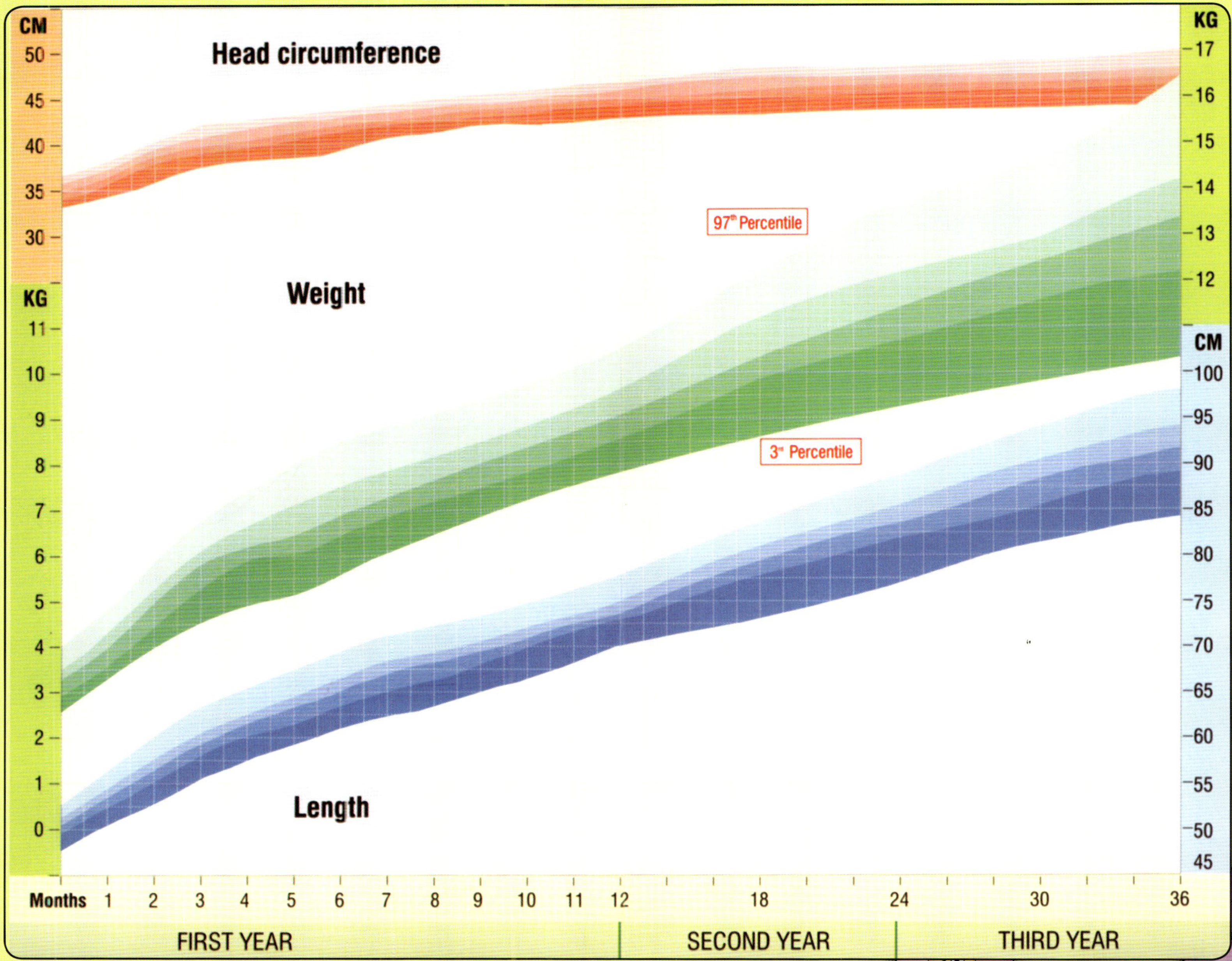

Paste copy of birth certificate

Immunization schedule

(Adopted from International Recommendations)

Vaccination Schedule			
Age	**Vaccine**	**Approx. Due Date**	**Date Given**
Birth	Hepatitis B 1st + OPV 0 dose		
1 month	Hepatitis B 2nd + BCG + OPV 1st		
2 months	DTaP/DPT 1st + OPV 2nd/IPV 1st + Hib 1st		
3 months	Pneumococcal 1st + Rotavirus 1st		
4 months	DTaP/DPT 2nd + OPV 3rd/IPV 2 nd + Hib 2nd		
5 months	Pneumococcal 2nd + Rotavirus 2nd		
6 months	DTaP/DPT 3rd + OPV 4th/IPV 3rd + Hib 3rd		
7 months	Hepatitis B 3rd + Pneumococcal 3rd + Rotavirus 3rd		
9 months	Measles		
1 year	Pneumococcal Booster Dose		
13 months	Hepatitis A 1st		
15 months	MMR (Tresivac/Priorix) + Chicken Pox 1st		
18 months	DTaP/DTP + Hib + OPV/IPV Booster		
19 months	Hepatitis A Booster		
2 years	Typhoid + M. Meningitis		
Any age	Influenza (every year)/Pneumococcal (Pneumo23)		
5 years	DTaP/DPT + OPV/IPV + Typhoid Booster, Chicken Pox II + MMR II		
8 years	Typhoid Booster (every 3 years lifelong)		
10 years	Tdap (every 10 years lifelong) + HPV for girls		
Any other	Yellow Fever/Japanese Encephalitis		
Any age	Rabies Prevention/Post Exposure		

BCG: Tuberculosis DPT: Diphtheria, Whooping cough, Tetanus; Hib: Haemophilus influenza b MMR: Measles, Mumps, Rubella, DPT vaccine may cause fever, irritability and injection lump.

Due dates mentioned are approximate dates after which the vaccine becomes due, a few days delay is allowed.

Vaccine details

Vaccines are live or killed organisms given at predetermined intervals for protection of the child from various deadly diseases by producing natural immunity. Although the schedule has been broadly given by the World Health Organization it can vary slightly from doctor to doctor.

BCG or Bacille Calmette Guerin is the vaccine given for protection against tuberculosis. It can be given right at birth but definitely within the first three months of age. It is given on the left shoulder into the layers of the skin. When given, it forms a small swelling which disappears in 10–15 minutes. It re-appears as a small boil after 4–6 weeks exuding 1–2 drops of pus and then healing gradually leaving a small scar by 3 months.

DPT or triple antigen as it protects against three diseases namely Diphtheria, Pertussis (whooping cough) and Tetanus. It has three primary doses given 4–6 week apart in the first year and two boosters given at 1½ and 5 years of age. It commonly causes fever along with a lump and swelling at the site of injection. Paracetamol drops and some sedative can be given. Rarely it may cause very high fever, convulsions and shock. DTaP is an alternative choice where the side effects are much less but the vaccine is expensive.

Oral polio drops are given at birth and then five doses of 2 drops each in the first year. Two boosters are given along with DPT at 1½ to 5 years of age. It may cause a very transient diarrhoea in some children. Inactivated Polio Vaccine (IPV) is now available in India which is in injectable form and is more effective.

Measles vaccine is given as a single dose at 9 months of age. It does not cause any reaction immediately; however, in some children it may cause fever and rashes after 5–10 days of the injection.

MMR is again a combination of three vaccines against Measles, Mumps and Rubella (German measles). It is given between 15 and 18 months of age. This may also lead to fever, mild rash and rarely jaw swelling after 5–10 days of injection. 2nd dose given at 5 years of age.

Typhoid vaccine can be of three types. The older vaccine was given every year and caused fever along with a lump and swelling at the site of injection. The new Vi antigen vaccine, though costlier, is given once every 3 years and has minimal side effects. Oral capsules are not available now.

Meningitis vaccine is to protect against one particular type out of the many causative organisms of meningitis (infection of the coverings of the brain). It is given once every 3 years and does not cause fever or local reactions.

Hepatitis means jaundice and can be of types A to E are water and food-borne and types B, C and D occur by injections, needle pricks, blood transfusions, etc. Vaccines are available only for prevention against A and B. Hepatitis A vaccine is given after 1 year of age in two doses 6 months apart. Hepatitis B is given in three doses – at birth, 1 and 6 months of age. A combination vaccine is now available also given in three doses. Usually there are no side-effects except for minor fever or local reaction in an occasional patient.

Hib vaccine is to protect the child against bacteria called Haemophilus influenza type b which is the common cause of meningitis, sore throat pneumonia and ear infection in children below 6 years of age. The number of doses varies from 4 to depending on the age of starting the vaccine.

Tetanus toxoid vaccine is not required in children as they are already covered in their DPT doses. From 10 years of age onwards, ideally all children should be given a dose of Tdap every 10 years. It has Tetanus and small dose of Diphtheria and Pertussis antigen.

Rabies vaccine is not routinely given but can be considered if the child is in close contact with animals. Usually it is given after an episode of dog bite in five doses given at 0, 3, 7, 14, and 30 days.

Chicken pox vaccine is given after 1 year of age and second dose at 5 years. After the 13th birthday the two doses are given 4–6 weeks apart. There may be a slight fever and/or rash after 10–15 days of the injection.

Pneumococcal vaccine protects against invasive pneumococcal diseases like pneumonia, ear infections, bacteremia and meningitis. It should be given if one can afford it.

Rotavirus vaccine is an oral vaccine to protect against Rotavirus diarrhoea. It is the commonest cause of viral diarrhoea in children less than 5 years of age. The vaccine is given in two/three doses (depending on brand), 4–6 weeks apart.

HPV vaccine is the first vaccine which protects against cancer. Human Papiloma Virus is the causative agent for cancer of the cervix (part of uterus) and genital warts. It is given in three doses to girls and women from 10 to 45 years of age.

It is advisable to be in regular contact with your paediatrician and ask about the latest status of these vaccines and inquires about newer ones. It is worth the cost and mild side-effects if any of the diseases can be prevented.

Remember

- Vaccines are usually safe. The advantages far outweigh any risks associated with immunization.
- Although properly given, vaccines may not give absolute protection from the disease.
- Mild cough, running nose and fever are not indications for delaying the due dose.
- Delay in one dose by a couple of weeks does not mean that the schedule has to be repeated from the beginning.

An injection on time saves nine.

Effective discipline

- Use a form of discipline that you feel right and works for you.
- Keep fiddly fingers and busy bodies busy.
- Have sensible expectations. A child cannot behave like an adult.
- Don't over-discipline. Don't fight over trivial matters.
- Say 'yes' more often than 'no'. Suggest alternatives.
- Take time to explain things.
- Don't ever compare a child to brothers, sisters or neighbours.
- All children are different and want to be treated as individuals. Give equal attention to each child in the family.
- Don't correct in front of people.
- Be consistent, otherwise the child is confused and loses faith.
- Understand that the child does not purposely try to make you mad. It just happens.
- Don't be put off on being asked 'silly' questions. The child will stop asking and seek information elsewhere.
- Don't use baby talk – he takes that as proper pronunciation.
- Encourage and reward the good. Ignore the undesired.
- When you mean it, say it with conviction and see it through.
- An occasional smack will let the child know where the limits lie.
- Avoid no-win situations. Be quick to retreat when losing.
- Remember, tension at home, conflicting opinions and parental point scoring sabotage effective discipline.
- If home is happy and secure, never be afraid to be firm. The adults of tomorrow will be happier and healthier if the parents of today are firmly in charge.

Remember that a child does not need to tell you that he cannot thrive without lots of love and understanding. Also, he does appreciate what you do for him even though he does not thank you.

Early schooling

Pre-school attended ....

Joined on .... Teacher's name ....

First day ....

....

....

Interview given in schools ....

....

Selected in ....

....

Fees deposited ....

Started going to big school ....

From ....

Teachers ....

Principal ....

First day ....

....

....

Friends ....

....

....

Further schooling ....

....

....

Injury prevention

A perfect example of minority rule is a baby in the house.

Now that there is a tiny human being who is unaware of the dangers lurking round the corner, you have to be very vigilant. Don't let your attention to be diverted especially when you are using potentially dangerous household products and electrical appliances. The most important point is never leave the toddler alone – in a room, driveway or park. On the other hand, also give him plenty of freedom for his experimentation. Next important point is 'set a safe example'. Teach the child about the safe and unsafe and explain why. To make your home safe get down to your knees and look around from the toddler's eyes. Here are a few practical hints.

- Start with the child itself. Buy non-inflammable clothes. Pants or shirt sleeves should not be too long. Use proper size shoes with non-slippery soles. Consider shoes without laces. Do not use necklaces (child may strangle himself), pointed ear-ring, etc.
- Cover all electrical outlets. Hide wires behind furniture or under the carpet so that the child does not chew on them.
- Check earthing on all sockets or install ELCBs on the mains. Un-plug electrical appliances when not in use.
- Keep all medicines, naphthalene balls, insect repellent mats, kerosene, phenyl, bindis, coins, button cells, sharp objects, nuts and bolts, etc. away. Teach the child not to put anything into his mouth till offered by an adult. Tell him not to run with his mouth full.
- Never give a plastic bag to a child to play with. Similarly, latex balloons if inhaled can cause choking.
- Keep dressing drawers locked and ash trays out of reach.
- All table lamps or naked bulbs should be out of reach.
- Install window guards/grills or lock them. No chair or stool should be kept near the windows, railing, parapet. Clear glass windows should have stickers so that the child does not walk through.
- Install door chain at the main door so that he does not go out on his own. Ideally all lower bolts of all doors should be removed – he may bolt himself in.
- Use short or no table-cloth. Remove glass top tables.
- While cooking, use the back burners of cooking range and turn the handle of the cooking utensil away from you.

- Do not hold a hot drink and the baby at the same time.
- Don't be in a hurry to answer the telephone or the door bell. Be sure the baby is safe or take her with you.
- While giving a bath, place the telephone receiver off hook so that there is no temptation to answer the call. A few seconds and a few inches of water are enough to drown a child.
- When you have to use the bathroom with a child in the house, leave the door open – a toddler may bolt you inside.
- Garbage bins should be kept outside the house.
- Place table fans and coolers out of reach. In winters use heaters of the blower type and not radiators. Exercising equipment, if any, should be in a separate room.
- Look for the child's hands when closing drawers or doors including that of the refrigerator.
- If put in a walker, the child should not be allowed near a step/stairs.
- House plants, especially cacti, should be outside the house.
- Never leave the child with a pet alone. Teach handling of pets safely.
- Extra precautions have to be taken if there are stairs in the house. Gate should be installed wherever there are more than three steps. At least the landings should be carpeted. The distance between the vertical bars of the railing should be maximum five inches.
- When going for an outing, start teaching street manners.
- In car rides, always use car seats, preferably fixed on the back seat. Never carry large toys, balloons as they might accidently obstruct vision. Do not allow the child to play with sharp toys when in motion. Never leave the child alone in the car, he might shift the gear to neutral.
- Before leaving the child in a park it is best to inspect the grass for broken glass, animal droppings, shrubs, etc. Keep the child away from tall grassy areas. Teach the child to maintain adequate distance from the swing. Water can be fun but all safety measures should be taken when in the pool.
- When sending the child alone keep a mental note of clothes the child is wearing.
- Do not write the child's name on his clothes, a child may trust a stranger who reads the name and pretends to be familiar with him.
- When choosing toys avoid those with removable small parts and strings longer than 6 inches. The toy should not have sharp pointed edges, projectile parts like arrows, electrical connections, coating of lead paint or have stickers (he may swallow and suffocate).
- Install smoke alarm if possible.
- Make yourself familiar with first-aid and emergency measures and keep necessary equipment ready.

A few selected names

For Girls

Aabashar
Aarohi
Aashita
Adhyasha
Adhira
Ahat
Aliya
Ammanat
Anahita
Anshika
Anandita
Ananya
Anibha
Anika
Anjum
Anshuka
Anushka
Anubha
Antara
Anija
Arpita
Arshiya
Arushi
Ashmi
Asis
Ayushi
Achala
Abhilya
Akhila
Amala
Anvita
Arundhati
Avani

Abhsa
Abholi
Adrika
Agharna
Ahalya
Aishani
Agrima
Ameya
Amodini
Anahita
Angarika
Anuva
Asavari
Banika
Bavleen
Bhavya
Bhoomika
Bhurvi
Bhaminee
Banita
Bakul
Bihu
Bahula
Chandrama
Charvi
Chaitali
Chimayi
Chitrali
Devangi
Devina
Diksha
Diya
Drishti

Dhriti
Dhvani
Dyuti
Devapriya
Ekta
Eshita
Enakshee
Erina
Falghunee
Falak
Garima
Geetika
Gurvisha
Gulal
Gazala
Harbani
Hashmita
Hershita
Hinna
Harita
Hemangi
Ilona
Isha
Ishani
Ipsita
Ikushu
Janmeet
Japneet
Jasneen
Jhanak
Jisha
Jhanavi
Jhoomar

Kaasha
Kashika
Katyani
Kavya
Khyati
Khyati
Kiya
Kundnika
Kaamakshee
Kuranjee
Keshi
Keya
Kokila
Kamakshi
Kankana
Kaumudi
Kimaya
Kundana
Kunjana
Kuntala
Kurangi
Lavanya
Loboni
Lipika
Lola
Latika
Manastha
Manya
Mehak
Mehar
Mridul
Malika
Madhul

Manjari
Medini
Mehal
Minal
Minati
Mohana
Mohita
Mudita
Neelabja
Neymat
Niharika
Nimisha
Nishika
Nishna
Nivita
Noor
Nundrisha
Nandana
Neelakshi
Neepa
Nishita
Nitya
Nityapriya
Niyati
Ojaswinee
Ojaswita
Omana
Palakh
Palvika
Parikshita
Piyu
Praachi
Pragya
Pravleen
Purva
Putul
Paridhi
Parnika
Pavani
Paranhita
Raag
Rachita
Rachla
Ratnika
Rhea
Rikhia
Ritika
Roli
Ruaab
Rubina
Ruhani
Riddhi
Rudra
Rukmi
Rijuta
Ritambhara
Ramani
Ramita
Riti
Ranjini
Saanchi
Saadhika
Sagrika
Sahiba
Sajneet
Saakshi
Sanah
Sanjam
Shaina
Sonalika
Sarah
Sarvari
Shagufa
Shagun
Shambhavi
Shireen
Shivangi
Shrankhala
Shreyanshi
Srishti
Shubhi
Shuchi
Snehal
Somya
Siyona
Silona
Sraavani
Stuti
Sukhmani
Sukriti
Sumedha
Sonakshi
Suvira
Siddhi
Sandhita
Sangya
Shubha
Sitaanshu
Saguna
Sahila
Sajala
Samhita
Sanchita
Snigdha
Stavita
Suhina
Tanvi
Tanya
Taranjeet
Tarini
Tejasvini
Tushna
Taranginee
Tulika
Tarunika
Tejshree
Tushita
Tanika
Tanuka
Tarjini
Tapasi
Tapoti
Teesta
Udita
Umang
Unnati
Urmika
Urmaya
Utpala
Urvi
Urshita
Urshila
Urmi
Varada
Varnika
Vedika
Vidhi
Vidisha
Vidushi
Vinati
Vandita
Vidula
Vanya
Vyomika
Vanaja
Varuni
Vela
Veni
Vijul
Wamika
Yashna
Yashila
Yakshini
Zareen
Zarina

For Boys

Aadit
Agrim
Archit
Abheek
Akshat
Akshit
Akul
Amol
Anamitra
Anant
Ananya
Anchit
Aniket
Anirbaan
Appan
Anshul
Archishman
Archit
Arihant
Arsh
Arush
Ashwat
Atreya
Abhinav
Abhirath
Abhirup
Achal
Achintya
Aryan
Adheesh
Ajitesh
Akhil
Amey
Ambar
Amolak
Atulya

Avaneesh
Ayushmaan
Adil
Agriya
Ainesh
Arnav
Amogh
Anmol
Arjit
Arav
Aryaman
Bhavya
Budhil
Bodhan
Badal
Chirag
Chirayu
Chittesh
Devang
Divij
Divyansh
Daman
Dhanesh
Ekalavya
Gandharv
Gaurang
Hersh
Harit
Hiresh
Harshit
Ishan
Indraneel
Jaiveer
Jivitesh
Kanan
Karandit

Kaustubh
Kesar
Konal
Kritin
Krish
Kshitij
Kadamb
Kanak
Kamran
Kamod
Kanad
Kanha
Kanu
Kedar
Keyur
Kinshuk
Kunja
Lakshay
Madhav
Madhur
Manik
Mehul
Manan
Mihir
Milind
Magan
Mahin
Mahish
Mainak
Madhup
Malay
Malhar
Mani
Misal
Mitul
Mohajit

Mohal
Mohul
Moulik
Murag
Nakul
Naman
Nihal
Nachiket
Niket
Nimish
Natesh
Nayan
Neelesh
Nilay
Nipun
Nirajit
Nirmay
Nirau
Niropam
Nishad
Nishant
Nishok
Ojas
Ojal
Pallab
Paranjay
Poojit
Paarth
Pragun
Pulak
Pranav
Pulkit
Pulin
Puru
Pratul
Pritish

Palaash
Param
Parjat
Paritosh
Payas
Prabhaas
Prabal
Prachur
Pradyot
Pradyum
Prajit
Pranit
Pratul
Praval
Pravir
Rahil
Rituparn
Ratul
Ribhu
Riju
Ritam
Rixit
Rasik
Ruchir
Rudr
Rajit
Rasul
Rijul
Rushil
Rohan

Rochan
Raag
Sahaj
Sahil
Samar
Samarth
Sambhav
Sanjit
Sankalp
Sangam
Sarvpriya
Shaurya
Shikhar
Shivam
Shivay
Shiven
Shobhit
Shourijya
Shrey
Shubhang
Siddhant
Sohil
Sumer
Soumil
Srijan
Sumanyu
Sushant
Suveer
Sachit
Shaunak

Sunam
Sovan
Shireesh
Sumitr
Sunand
Suparu
Sushen
Sushrut
Sachet
Sambit
Samvit
Sanat
Sanchay
Shrenik
Snehin
Shaksham
Tahir
Tejaswi
Tanay
Tunav
Taarank
Taareesh
Tuhin
Tushaar
Tarik
Udayan
Utkarsh
Utkrisht
Utpal
Vansh

Vardaan
Vasu
Vibhor
Vikhyat
Viren
Vitesh
Vyar
Vandan
Vibhakar
Vibhu
Vidhu
Vinamr
Viraj
Vishnesh
Vitthal
Vyom
Vyomesh
Vanjit
Vibhas
Vikesh
Viresh
Yogeesh
Yatin
Yadu
Yashodhar
Yajas
Yajil
Yashas
Zain

There are several websites that list baby names.

About the authors

Dr Arun Wadhwa is a reputed child specialist practising in South Delhi for more than 20 years. He completed MBBS & MD (Paediatrics) from Safdarjung Hospital, Delhi. At present he is associated with Max Hospital Saket and Apollo Hospital Sarita Vihar, New Delhi. He is the advisor to *Child* magazine and a number of schools and companies.

Dr Taruna, his wife, is a practising radiologist and ultrasonologist working for the last 17 years. She completed MBBS from Lady Hardinge Medical College & MD (Radiodiagnosis) from Maulana Azad Medical College in Delhi.

They both run a private clinic in Greater Kailash II of South Delhi, India.